SEA SUMS

Joy N. Hulme

Illustrated by Carol Schwartz

Hyperion Books for Children
New York

Printed in Hong Kong by South China Printing Company (1988) Ltd.

First Edition

1 3 5 7 9 10 8 6 4 2

The artwork for each picture is prepared using Designer's Gouache.
This book is set in 16-point Oz Handicraft.
Designed by Joann Hill Lovinski.

Library of Congress Cataloging-in-Publication Data

Hulme, Joy N.
Sea Sums / Joy Hulme ; illustrated by Carol Schwartz——1st ed.
p.   cm.
ISBN 0-7868-0170-0 (trade)——ISBN 0-7868-2142-6 (lib. bdg.)
1. Addition—Juvenile literature. 2. Subtraction—Juvenile
literature.   [1. Addition. 2. Subtraction.] I. Schwartz, Carol, 1954— ill.
II. Title.
QA115.H85 1996
513.2'11—dc20
95–5935

For all budding marine biologists.
Special thanks to Chuck Worden for his encouragement and assistance
——J. H.

For Paul and Blaise
——C. S.

In an underwater grotto,
Where the sea is warm and blue,
There are creatures to be counted
In every shape and hue.
We'll have a great adventure,
An encounter face-to-face,
While we're adding and subtracting
In this coral-reefy place.

A giant clamshell opens up
To let its mantle spread
In brilliant purples, greens, and blues
Down on the ocean bed.

One siphon sucks in briny brew,
One siphon spouts it out.
Two siphons pump seawater through
While food is filtered out.

$$1 \text{ siphon} + 1 \text{ siphon} = 2 \text{ siphons}$$

Two triggerfish may choose to dine
On fresh-cracked crabs at suppertime.
If one eats **three** and one eats **two**
Five crabs will disappear from view.
'Cause triggerfish, each time they eat,
Must grind up shells as well as meat.
Then afterward they'll swim away
To look for other kinds of prey.

$3 \text{ crabs} + 2 \text{ crabs} = 5 \text{ crabs}$

When foes approach two surgeonfish
Four scalpels pop up with a swish
To stab an enemy that might
Decide to try to take a bite.

But when the coast is clear of foes,
The blades can just as quickly close.
And then those surgeons swim away,
No weapons showing as they play.

4 scalpels – 4 scalpels = 0 scalpels

Two spiny, spiky urchins
Come creeping from a cave;
Three others rest next to the reef,
Where they just point and wave.

But if **one** more moved into view
Then ***six*** would be the sum.
Numbers just keep adding up
When other urchins come.

2 urchins $+ 3$ urchins $+ 1$ urchin $= 6$ urchins

Three purple pipes are pumping
Some sea stew through their pores;
Four yellow tubes sip dinner
Through hollow corridors;

Two vases sway in ocean broth
And soak their supper up;
Nine sponges drink in nourishment
Without a glass or cup.

3 sponges $+ 4$ sponges $+ 2$ sponges $= 9$ sponges

One lionfish is bristling
With pointed, poison spines;
Two others flutter from a cove
Like feathered porcupines.

16

Around their faces, frilly fins
Spread like a lion's mane.
When **one** swims off to find some food,
Two fluffy fish remain.

1 lionfish + 2 lionfish – 1 lionfish = 2 lionfish

A booby swoops through a lagoon
And gulps a *six*-fish meal,
Then surfaces to fly away
With *two* more in its bill.

A frigate makes a snack attack
And grabs those **two** away,
So the booby only gets the **six**
It swallowed in the bay.

6 fish $+ \, 2$ fish $- \, 2$ fish $= 6$ fish

Coral polyps spread their rings
Of tentacles below.
Ten are golden, *ten* are green,
And *ten* are white like snow.

But when an ebbing tide retreats,
Exposing them to air,
Thirty circles close up tight
And show no fringes there.

10 polyps $+$ 10 polyps $+$ 10 polyps $= 30$ polyps

Two barnacles inside their shells
Stand on their heads to eat
As **twenty-four** fine-feathered legs
Kick in a seafood treat.

But when one pulls its legs inside
And shuts its two-part lid
Twelve legs will stay to swing and sway
While **twelve** are safely hid.

$$24 \text{ legs} - 12 \text{ legs} = 12 \text{ legs}$$

A stingray digs **two** sandy clams,
Down on the ocean floor,
Then plows around until it finds
One . . . two . . . three . . . **four** more.

24

It chews **three** clams for breakfast,
And crunches **three** for brunch—
So all the clams are gobbled up,
And **none** are left for lunch.

2 clams + 4 clams - 3 clams - 3 clams = 0 clams

We haven't yet begun to count
A fraction of the full amount
Of ocean animals that grow
In coral caverns down below.
In underwater grottoes
Numbers seldom stay the same.
Adding and subtracting
Is a never-ending game.

A CORAL REEF is a complex community of ocean animals and plants found only in warm, clear, shallow water. The reef is built up from the ocean floor by corals that have left behind their white, stony skeletons. They form all sorts of complicated shapes—towers, tunnels, caves, and cavities—in which a wide variety of colorful creatures make their homes. Sponges, anemones, and algae stick to surfaces. Worms, lobsters, and crabs move in and out of small holes; octopuses and eels hide in larger caves. Brightly patterned fish swim in and out of rocky ravines and through ferny forests of waving sea fans. Some hide in cracks and crevices. Stingrays ripple along the sandy bottom. Sharks and barracudas cruise around the edges of the reef, watching for an opportunity to grab a bite to eat. Sea birds soar and swoop over the shallow lagoons and nest on islands and cays.

Every variety of reef life needs nourishment. Some animals feed on the algae and seaweed that grow in the ocean. Others filter their food from the nutritious seawater. Some fish eat other fish. All day and all night, an intricate interaction of plants and animals takes place on the coral reef.

When the huge, scalloped, two-part shell of the GIANT CLAM opens, the beautiful *mantle* is visible. The rich color comes from millions of tiny one-celled plants called algae that live just under the surface. Using the sun's energy, seawater nutrients, and clam waste products, these algae manufacture enough food to share with their clam hosts. A siphon system pumps seawater in through one opening and out through another so the clam can filter out small bits of food.

Many varieties of TRIGGERFISH live in coral-reef waters. The first spine on the dorsal fin serves as an unusual protective weapon. It can be raised up or bent down flat, as needed. When the sturdy, barbed spine is lifted, a small second spine, called the trigger, moves forward to lock it in place. The upright spine can kill an enemy that bites down on it, discouraging most predators from making a meal of the triggerfish. The needle also comes in handy as a hook to hold the animal firmly in the narrow coral crannies where it hides. After anchoring itself, the fish inflates its loose belly skin until it is wedged so tightly that no predator can get it out. With its powerful jaws and strong, sharp teeth, a triggerfish crunches coral, crabs, urchins, mollusks, tube worms, and brittle stars.

When a foe comes too close to a SURGEONFISH, its scalpels snap open like jackknife blades. A quick swish of the tail delivers a discouraging slash to the enemy. The yellowtail surgeon, also called the flagtail or regal tang, feeds on algae. Some surgeons eat both living and dead coral.

The SEA URCHIN looks like an inside-out pincushion. The spiny, pivoting points protect the animal and help it move. Tube feet with sucking disks on the ends stick out through holes between the spines. Longer than the spines, the feet are used as feeling organs. They also help the urchin move about, and they push algae and kelp into the animal's mouth, located on its undersurface. Urchins live on the ocean floor near rocky shores. They bite seaweed from the rocks using their teeth and powerful scraping jaws.

Adult SPONGES are always *sessile*, or attached by a base, to rocks or other solid objects on the ocean floor. They are nourished by microscopic bits of food and oxygen contained in the water constantly being pumped through the numerous pores and tubes that make up the sponge's body. Food is absorbed into and waste products are expelled from the sponge's hollow center. Sponges grow in warm, shallow waters and come in many forms and colors.

Swimming slowly in submarine pools and caverns, LIONFISH protect their territory from intruders. Their beautiful fins are really deadly weapons, used for attack as well as for defense. Each spine is lined with grooves containing a lethal poison similar to cobra venom. A single puncture can cause excruciating pain.

FRIGATE BIRDS and BOOBIES are frequently found together, dipping and diving for seafood dinners on tropical coral-reef islands and shores. Frigate birds have extremely long wings, forked tails, and powerful breast muscles. They hiss as they dive, then carefully peck up food from the surface of the water. Frigates must stay dry because their feathers have no oily coating to repel water. If the birds get wet, they will quickly sink and drown. Frigate birds often snatch prey from the bills of other birds, especially boobies.

Boobies, with their broad, blue- or red-webbed feet, are designed for swimming on or under the sea surface. They rise to great heights and dive swiftly straight down, folding their wings together just before entering the water. They stay submerged for some time, catching and swallowing fish. As the heavy-bellied booby surfaces and tries to fly away, a frigate bird is likely to attack.

A CORAL polyp (PO-lip) is a simple animal consisting of a tiny, bony cup with a ring of tentacles around the mouth. Numerous coiled whips of stinging cells lash out when edible animals (crustaceans, newly hatched fish, sea worms) touch the tentacles. This paralyzes the prey, which is then drawn into the polyp's opening and digested. Corals generally feed at night and close up in the daytime. When exposed to air, the tentacles retract so they won't dry out. Dead polyps leave their skeletons behind and, inch by inch, form all sorts of fanciful shapes, such as fans, whips, and branching horns.

When first hatched, BARNACLE larvae have six legs and one eye and can swim. At the next stage in their lives, they have twelve feet, twelve feelers, and two eyes. Then the eyes disappear, and the feelers become suckers that secrete a strong cement with which the barnacles attach themselves, head down, to ships, docks, shells, or rocks, for the rest of their lives. They surround themselves with limestone cones shaped like volcano craters. Inside the opening on top, a vertical valve opens to allow feathery legs to reach out and kick food inside.

A STINGRAY, or stingaree, has a flattened shape that ripples like a swirling cape. The pectoral fins are like big, broad wings that flap as the animal swims. The stingrays also use these oversize fins to find food, beating the fins on the seabed to unearth worms and clams. Strong, flat teeth act like nutcrackers to crush food. A barbed, poisonous spine, or stinger, is located near the base of a stingray's whiplike tail. One quick swing of the tail can inflict a terribly painful, sometimes fatal wound. The stinger is used mostly as a protective device.

Other coral-reef animals found in Sea Sums:

Pages 4–5: (*clockwise from top right*) squarespot basslets, sponge, brain coral, surgeonfish, staghorn coral, blue sea star, sponge, feather star, giant clam, Meyer's butterfly fish, orange-lined triggerfish

Pages 8–9: calico crabs with triggerfish

Pages 12–13: (*left to right*) table coral, sea fan coral, staghorn coral with urchins

Pages 14–15: longnose tilefish with sponges

Pages 24–25: (*left to right*) stingray, juvenile sweetlips, sea horse, branching coral

Pages 26–27: (*clockwise from top right*) lemon peel angelfish, soft coral, ornate butterfly fish, purple staghorn coral, sponge, feather star, barnacle, fairy basslet, urchin, branching coral, blue and gold angelfish, threadfin basslet, table coral, soft coral